Flowing
with
Milk
and
Honey

Poems to **propel you**
towards the
Promised Land

by

Julian Palmer

Julian Palmer
Contact:
Instagram: www.instagram.com/tha.po3t/
Mailing Address:
P.O. Box 823
McKinney, TX 75070

ISBN: 978-1-936497-48-5

To all the experiences God has blessed me with,
and allowed me to suffer through for my betterment;
thank you for supplying me with the inspiration
to help express myself, and hopefully inspire others.
And to my mother and father for never giving up
on this ol' goofball:
I love you both.

Contents

"My hope for you is that these words will leave you brimming with

Conviction,
and a desire to attach yourself to the

Uplifting Promises
of Christ. I also pray your

Thoughts and Feelings
don't drown out your desire to be free. To my readers, God loves you, and so do **I**."

The _**Author's Account**_
Explanations detailing the mind behind and/or what each poem means to me

---

Conviction

"May you be inspired
to make a change
(with God as your guide)
and/or find the strength
to keep pushing forward"

Life Is Like a War Zone

Life is like a war zone
Steeped in fire, while shells rain down on your dome
You were handed the living water, but left it at your "home"
Left gnashing at your teeth, as fire peels away at your bones
The fire flickers
As smoke gets thicker
A closed window, now you're blind
Landmines explode, but it's not a Holy Land
Pierced by the Holy Spear; it leaves untainted blood on your
hands
"Whose blood was spilled?" you ask
To get to safety, such a task
You struggle to stand,
You pant, you gasp
You've fainted
Your company begins to flee
THEY see, your wounds have gotten too deep
A cruel reality enters your mind:
Beware the company you keep
Left dying, and alone
The light descends to reach you
The years you lived, so few
Life <u>WAS</u> like a warzone

Author's Account

The line "steeped in fire while shells rain down on your dome" serves a double purpose: shells are large projectiles that cause widespread damage when fired, but within the poem's biblical context, you break apart "shell" and you've got "s-**hell**-s rain[ing] down". This is meant to paint a picture of the rapture, and how God promised the world would end in flames (and not a flood as it did in Noah's time). The "left gnashing at your teeth..." line further adds to the depiction of hell as detailed in **Luke 13:28**

"land mines explode, but it's not a Holy Land" serves a double purpose as landmines break the ground apart when they explode, leaving the ground full of holes (or holey). As well, this world is so full of sin that it can't come close to being compared to the Holy Land.

"Pierced by the Holy Spear; it leaves untainted blood on your hands" read all at once sounds like you're saying "pierced by the Holy Spirit..." ; intentional as the line itself is symbolic of salvation: being "pierced" [or having the Holy Spirit become a part of you], places his untainted blood [Jesus' blood] on our hands [an artistic way of saying that his blood is covering us]. The subsequent "whose blood was spilled?" line is there to have you, the reader, ask yourself that question and ponder who the first person to be slaughtered in the warfare was, and the significance of His death.

"Your company begins to flee **THEY** see your wounds have gotten too deep;" playing on the war imagery, a military unit is called a company and as well, the people you surround yourself in the apocalyptic setting of war will likely desert you as they have not the faith to stand up to and suffer for the cause of Christ.

Palmer, 11

"Wounds have gotten too deep" depicts physical battle scars, as well as the emotional (and sometimes physical) wounds one receives from being a believer.

The compassion I carry for people births the anger, frustration, and sadness I feel in knowing that some will not make it into heaven. This poem was written in the hopes that people realize the reality of living in a world of sin, so they don't die in this war not knowing who the Lord is and what the Bible means.

For the love of...

A promise never kept, only forgotten
Cindy's eyes, you always get lost in
Pray this guise, you may drop and
Start anew
Start fresh
What to do?
An endless test, thoughts run into walls
Runnin' just to fall, you reach; never tall enough
To get over, and get your answers
Drop your pencils, drop your weapon, it's over
Into the machine you go, propelled
Like a pinball
The ball falls: Happy New Year!
New fears introduce themselves
New vices touch the shelves
Sin in these eyes
A red dot on your forehead:
You're dead
Chasing the bull; it got you killed
You're not thrilled that it's finally finished
'Cause your happy nest was diminished
A grimace:
Pride had you loving your "old-fashioned ways"
Dressed up your spirit, but you can't fool His gaze
Thought you was cool with those chains, but you're still just
A Slave
Life was electric... at least it was
Before you got tazed
Out the machine, like money

You fall to the ground

Palmer, 13

Author's Account

One of my favorites for all the hidden meanings

The allure of what's immoral can be compared to the feeling you get when drawn to someone you know is bad for you: you love the way they look at you, and the way they make you feel, but are unaware of the vitality they're stealing from you. You get lost in "Cindy's eyes"(a play on the word "sin"), while "she" kills you from the inside out.

"Into the machine you go, propelled Like a pinball, The ball falls: Happy New Year" serves a double purpose as our minds sometimes move erratically, not unlike [the ball in] a pinball machine. The "machine" also characterizes the soulless patterns we participate in as cogs in this crooked world (I also liken my thoughts to a pinball bouncing around when writing these poems). The "Happy New Year" line refers to how humanity gets so caught up in this cycle of repetitive sins that before we know it, we're in a new year dealing with the same issues as before.

"Sin in these eyes A red dot on your forehead: You're dead Chasing the bull; it got you killed " is the repetition of the previous "Cindy's eyes" with its literal meaning. The next line serves a double purpose as, like the letter "i", there's a dot above it, with red signifying blood. As well, certain guns attach to a sight that allow the shooter to shine a red dot onto its target for precision aim. "Chasing the bull; it got you killed"; typically the bull chases after the matador, but in this instance humanity is chasing the metaphorical "bull", being used here to represent good fortune.

This sentence together can be heard as "chasing the bullet got you killed" which piggybacks off of the gun imagery used previously.

"'Cause your happy nest was diminished" is meant to be read as "happiness was diminished" as living in the "machine" robs you of the feeling. Separating it as happy, and the word nest gives way to the image of living in a world where you piece together something similar to joy, but in death, see that "nest" shaken, and broken apart.

"Pride had you loving your "old-fashioned ways" Dressed up your spirit, but you can't fool His gaze Thought you was cool with those chains…"; is all a comparison of biblical concepts to clothing. Pride leads many to be arrogant not just in actions [their "old-fashioned ways"], but in their outward appearance as well. As such, they're "dressed up" in that pride which would have many believe them to be better off, but in reality, God knows how lowly they truly are. ".. cool with them chains" compares the chains some wear around their neck, to the ones that keep people in bondage. Additionally, chains can be seen as a symbol of status so you're a slave to what the world perceives is "wealth" as well.

"I titled this "For the Love of…" as a I wanted you [the reader] to fill in the blank with whatever vice, whatever immoral desire that you've fallen in love with, and within these words possibly see if **you've** become part of the machine. Fame, fortune, none of it matters in the grand scheme of it all.

Storm Chaser

Storm chaser
Storm chaser
Your curiosity
Never satisfies the urge
To pursue
A goal from which you never waver
Storm chaser
Storm chaser
You'd risk your life for the chase
A tornado touches down
Lightning strikes the ground
A fatal kiss
Excitement creeps upon your face
Storm chaser
Storm chaser
A storm rolls in
Your insatiable thirst for adventure
Has wind peeling at your skin
Running headfirst into danger,
You don't realize your mistake
That fatal kiss stings like a viper
"Lightning" strikes, just like the snake
Storm chaser
Storm chaser

Palmer, 16

Author's Account

The storm is symbolic of a culture that's only focused on personal gain, or rather, the concept of personal gain itself. Lightning here represents the devil within the storm, while the other byproducts of said storm are the difficulties and signs that many ignore on the path to their inevitable destruction.

Upon observing the world we live in, I wrote this to detail what a "storm chaser" is, and to discourage people from the lifestyle. I pray it might even persuade those who live said life to leave the storm before "lightning" strikes them down sooner than they'd have hoped.

A reality check
Better bounce before it snaps your neck,
Show's over
It's the finale, so don't miss the details
Pay attention:
The
Playboy chases affection, not a feeling. Feeds his erection with thoughts that never fill the hole in his heart. Sin penetrates; impregnates his soul with sorrow. He played the world's game of "Life" and lost: Here Lies No Love
Wages
The stockbroker makes, they pack his pockets with paper, and pride; "KA-CHING", the sound? his soul breaks. The market rises and falls, ebbs and flows, high society, cocaine comes spilling out his nose. His heart gains, his mind loses the rest. Lamborghini, in a crash, he chose the wrong thing to invest.
Of
All the things to wish for, you asked for a painting presented by a liar. He rattled off lies like a snake, rocked you to sleep like a baby, you got a snapshot of a fake; why didn't you ask the buyer? You're left bleeding on an empty canvas of concrete, furious, blood filled with venom, spills out and leaks on your denim; this game you've been playing like the boy, ends in defeat. In your ears ring one final
Sin-tence
The sirens cut it off - your bill is due. No refunds. The reward for your fatal independence
Is Death

Palmer, 18

Author's Account

"A reality check
Better bounce before it snaps your neck,
Show's over
It's the finale so don't miss the details
Pay attention:"

The phrase " reality check" is used in situations where someone needs to be reminded of what's going on in the real world, outside of their opinions and emotions. It's followed by ,"Better bounce before you snap your neck", which is a harsh way of saying that if you don't escape the realm of "feeling instead of thinking," then you **will** perish. "Show's over" is symbolic of death, while also being a tie into the concept of reality TV. "It's the finale so you'd better not miss the details" preludes the remainder of the poem as it's a call to listen [read] carefully, while further adding into the television imagery. Lastly, "pay attention" ties into the concept of finance as "check", "[check] bounce" and "pay" are all money-related terminology. The concepts of money and television here are referenced as both are things that draw us into the world, and out of our [your] purpose.

The Playboy
A symbol of lust; the phrases used are purposefully chosen as they're sexual in nature i.e. "feeds his erection...", "the hole...", "sin penetrates, impregnates...". "Here Lies No Love" spells out the crux of this lifestyle as although it all may feel good, it leaves you feeling empty as nothing can truly replace love.

The Stockbroker
A symbol of greed, and a lack of self-control. "Rises and falls, ebbs and flows" is representative of the money market, and how (in the world of fame and fortune), there's truly no telling when

Palmer, 19

your 15 minutes of fame is up. "Lamborghini, in a crash, he chose the wrong thing to invest"; the Lamborghini is a symbol of wealth so in crashing it, his money and status are gone along with it. As well, because he chose to invest in what was temporary, he dies with nothing.

The devil is the liar presenting this false painting of what our hearts [flesh] desire life to be, and the buyer is Jesus; the one who bought our salvation when he died for us on the cross.

Taken directly out of **Romans 6:23**, with the underlined words being the first half of the verse itself, I wrote this to wake us all up, so that we might see ourselves within the playboy, or stockbroker and make a change, that when the time comes to pass on, our (metaphorical) debt is expunged and we're able to reach the Promised Land.

the snake snickers as i sin
as i fight a battle i cannot win
agents of death, let slip a grin
a ceaseless slumber, then life begins
Arise!
at the crossroads, but you can't pursue both sides
this ride that is life, your choice decides who dies
Foolish to think that your disdain holds so much weight, your
enemy cries
with hatred in my eyes, i surmise it's my flesh that i despise:
Believe no other lies
All that's left is contrast:
Black envies white, humanity envies purity
Our existence is a sickness; a prescription,
God's the remedy
Pressure in heat, steady your feet
Let pride melt away like ice
Remember you've been chosen
A righteous heart is never frozen
Let it beat

Again and again
Live a life like the wise
With the Bible as your belief:
Reassurance and relief
Eyes so wide that reside in truth
Like Job, Like David, Like Ruth
Pursue Christ!

Palmer, 21

Author's Account

The poem in its entirety is a metaphor for being spiritually asleep, or being spiritually awake. To be asleep is to pursue the devil: to continue fighting the battle of good versus evil alone while not reaching for the hand of God to make it easier. To be awake is to hate your flesh enough that you allow the **Lord** to supply you with the strength needed to choose what's righteous, instead of trying to find it yourself. Contrast being the only thing that's left reflects the fact that within the battle of good and evil, you either decide to stay asleep, or choose to be awake; "you can't pursue both sides".

There's a lot of conversation to be had about rebuking the sinner, and making them see their errors. While I did decide to rebuke in some parts, I primarily wanted to offer encouragement in the hopes that you latch onto these words and make it your unshakeable goal to "live a life like the wise": spending every second pursuing Christ, and Him alone.

To the backslider

"Nobody's perfect";
Not a way to live your life
Blatant ignorance such as that,
Precedes a lifetime of strife
Time, it ticks on
To you it's just a suggestion
"I've got time, I've got time"
It's up. You've missed the entire lesson
Lessons learned, there are none
For you'd rather have your fun
"One life to live,
No need to forgive"
You forget, while your companions, they outlive you
YOU are the problem
YOU'VE lost your pace
Don't blame it on the devil
YOU fail, while he bellows in your face
"Time is winding up";
You whine
While Heaven comes to earth
Your bones, they turn to ashes
As the world begins rebirth. One final lesson precedes the plight:
Get right, before you see the light!

Palmer, 23

Author's Account

At some point in our lives we've all been, or are currently plagued by some addiction that's drawn us away from God. We try to resist the temptation, but in our flesh we continually fail. This poem is for all those who know better, WANT to do better outwardly, but still find themselves willfully following their heart instead of the Holy Spirit.

My prayer to those who have backslidden or are backsliding is that you stop making empty claims, and instead make the decision to commit to a change.

Palmer, 24

The Human Condition

A door opens:
Excitement,
Grandeur,
Ostentation

We enter

Blood's spilled like liquor
It's consumed, but never savored
They think they know its taste,
But in their confusion, they read the wrong label:
One brings forth true peace, one makes you unstable
Like an addictive drug
Our lives depend on its effects
How it would affect our souls
Which pill do you reach for when insanity pollutes your mind
like the filth you consume pollutes your body?
YOU'VE GOT TO GET A HANDLE ON YOUR LIFE!
A handle
Which door will you reach for? Is it too late?
A door closes
Where am I?
Dying,
Death,
Gone

Palmer, 25

Author's Account

Another one of my favorite poems for all its imagery and intention:

"**E**xcitement, **G**randeur, and **O**stentation"; the first letter of each word taken out spells EGO, which I feel is the primary problem humanity faces. Our pride, our arrogance, and propensity to think we're owed anything keeps us from humbling ourselves enough to follow Christ.

"Blood's spilled like liquor"; the blood spilled is Jesus': vitally important to the believer, but to the rest of the world it means about as much as cheap liquor spilled on the floor.

"It's consumed, but never savored, They think they know its taste"; the world hears the Gospel, they "consume" it, but they don't cherish or value its worth. They believe that knowledge of the flesh trumps what the Bible says is true, and conclude they "know better" because of it.

"But in their confusion, they read the wrong label"; the world is convinced that immorality and promiscuity is the "good wine" and that in drinking of its cup, they'll achieve the "buzz" they're looking for. In reality, they've confused the "temporary fix" of sin with the genuine power one gets from drinking of the Lord's supply. Confusion, as stated in **1st Corinthians 13:33**, is NOT of the Lord.

"One brings forth true peace, one makes you unstable"; drinking enough of real alcohol will make you unstable, inversely, the things which God supplies only serve to clear the mind.

"Like an addictive drug, Your life depends on it , How it would affect your soul"; has a double meaning with the continuation of drug use imagery, while also comparing one's commitment to God (or the devil) with an addiction. In terms of drug use, you can become so addicted that you can't live without them (and even experience withdrawals), and biblically speaking your life after death [Heaven or hell] depends on who you're "addicted" to.

The door opening represents being born into a world full of EGO and sinfulness, with everything in between being the passage of life. The final few lines, "a door closes" to "dying, death, gone" not only relate back to the opening, but it concludes the story of life as well. After being presented with both sides, you're prompted with an insightful question: to choose the path of life, or death. In the end, we all must ask ourselves that question before the door closes.

Out the way

Your reputation precedes you
Headstrong, no one
No wisdom to concede to
Chase fun, feet run headfirst into trials
Been like this,
Sin like this,
Old age, in the crib, when walking down the aisle
Trade the stroller for a cane, yet you're still unable to find order
in your steps
A nursery, adultery: child gleams with gladness, hands move to
madness, tears of joy, tears of sadness, either way
A woman wept
Her son died, despite her teachings, he fell to pride, she tried and
tried
But never prayed
Plagued by emotion, cursing God as she visits the site where he
was laid
God paid a price
But we'd rather roll the dice with our lives: leave our husbands,
leave our wives off a decision that WE made
Never ask to be sure, only move because you're "certain"
God could've made your life a triumphant play,
But your flesh tripped on the curtain

A reminder of what happens when we don't get out the way

Palmer, 28

Author's Account

"Trade out the stroller for a **cane**, but you're still un**able** to find order in your steps"; a reference to Cain and Abel in the Bible, a story which details Cain murdering his brother Abel in cold blood out of jealousy. An apt reference as jealousy is an emotion that leads you to pursue what's not yours, while removing you from the calling on your life.

"A nursery, adultery: child gleams with gladness, hands move to madness, tears of joy, tears of sadness, either way, A woman wept": Within the nursery an infant learns to smile, leading a mother to cry tears of joy. On the other hand, she cries tears of sadness from finding out her husband's been unfaithful. Two concepts melded together in order to juxtapose the beauty of new life, versus the death of love, and how purity is lost in the time span between the two due to the interference of the flesh.

"Never ask to be sure, only move because you're "certain", God could've made your life a triumphant play, But your flesh tripped on the curtain"; is meant to be a wakeup call to those who take too much pride in their choice. In doing so, our free will continuously puts us at risk of "tripping over the curtain", which is to live outside of God's plan. God wants to bless us all, but so often our own "wits" get in the way of His wisdom.

We: our emotions, thoughts, feelings, etc. are the ONLY thing keeping us from being blessed and "highly favored". If we want to receive God's blessing, and be confident that we are within the realm of his protection

Palmer, 29

then we must swallow our pride, humble ourselves, and make way for the success of God's plan over our own.

Lukewarm

This world is dying
Eyes that've frozen over, unperturbed by lucifer's wicked words
Will soon be crying
Lying to God about promises they made
But didn't keep
Possessions surrender to flames
As lost souls continue to weep
Tears cannot save those committed to what's wicked,
Years they could've admitted fault and sought the Kingdom,
shaved off for like children, they couldn't behave
They burn to ash, overlooked by the few
Left looking towards the heavens asking:
"What did **I** do to deserve God's wrath?"
Your task was to sing in the church choir
To place prayers on new hires,
To guide those who had pennies to pay for salvation towards the
buyer
But you settled on being a liar
Opened your Bible only on Sunday
The rest of the week it lay next to your pile of vices, the prices of
which mean more to you than the blood shed for your soul that
was already dead
"Prayed up"
While you stayed up late, tempting the fate that befalls all those
who can't decide their master
At the chapel everyday, but everyday ignore your pastor
The cost of being lukewarm
Surrounded by the swarm

Author's Account

"Eyes that've frozen over…" is a reference to having a hardened heart, which is a state of unrepentance [as mentioned in the Bible, the reference being King Saul]. Just as Saul's **heart** was hardened making him a slave to his desires, the world's **eyes** too are frozen: glued onto what's wicked, unfazed by the enemy at work.

The line "They burn to ash, overlooked by the few" is directly pulled out of **1st Thessalonians** chapter **4** verses **16-18**. This line in specific draws from v. 17 which mentions all those left on this earth meeting with the Lord in the sky. This trickles directly into the next line where we're "looking towards the heavens asking...", as the tone is shifting from sadness for the sinner [the world] to dread for the lukewarm believer. They "deserve God's wrath" as they know enough of the bible to "pass" as a Christian, but don't cherish it enough to LIVE by it: this type of believer as mentioned in **Revelation 3: 15-16** is no good to God, deserving to be spat out of his mouth like tepid water. Subsequent lines serve as an exposé of the life of someone lukewarm: that being someone who knows God's plan for them, but follows their flesh instead.

"The cost of being lukewarm, Surrounded by the swarm"; the swarm being a piece of imagery, depicting a group of demons and sinners dragging the "believer" to hell.

It deeply wounds my soul knowing there are those who believe but don't **treasure** the salvation they have, opting to waste it on what's wicked. I solemnly hope, and pray that if you find yourself in these words that you'll fully repent, and work towards the will of God.

Palmer, 32

Father, Time

A scoured earth, hours slip through the hands of man, God's
counter can't clock wisdom in time
Fixed betwixt the ticks is a chance for change
Prompted to progress only by the promise of second-chances
While still fumbling the mere minutes
The many moments of missed opportunity
Never sever the wrist for the absence of watchfulness
Solely wish for peace in the present
A gift ungranted
Senses suffocate in the midst of quicksand
Once were wading
Now waiting to be displaced from pain
Stranded; the consequence for going against the grains
Mocked, as the clock continues to count down

A prayer:
Might hands rotate around 'till they've found what's wise
Before they strike

Palmer, 33

Author's Account

This is my favorite of the poems geared towards conviction as it combines all the elements I feel make a good poem: imagery, alliteration, wordplay, and an image that brings it all together. "Father, Time" represents the entity, and begging the Father for more time.

"...hours slip through the hands of man, God's **counter** can't **clock** wisdom in time". The image of an hourglass is presented at multiple points within this poem and, in this instance, it's meant to depict the sand within one literally (and metaphorically) slipping away from man, as his life slips from his body. We all move **counterclockwise** to God, which is to say we move opposite the direction he would have us to go. Additionally, God is perfect, we are not, therefore we are his counter: the opposite of him.

"Never sever the wrist for the absence of watchfulness" is my favorite line within the poem, being a reference to **Matthew 5:29**, a verse which details gouging one's eye out if it causes you to stumble (as it'd be better to lose **one** sinful appendage, than to have your **entire body** cast in hell). Watchfulness is the ability to discern the truth so the line itself is saying that man isn't willing to remove whatever appendage is guilty, despite not being as alert as he should be ["man" here is a blanket for humanity as a whole].

"Stranded; the consequence for going against the grains, Mocked..." A double entendre for going against the grains of sand within the hourglass, and a metaphor for working towards a goal opposite of what God's goal is for you [us]. We're mocked by satan, who laughs at our error(s), as he prepares to take our souls.

Palmer, 34

Uplifting Promises

"May you be overjoyed, and
become spirited when you see
what all God has for, and desires for you.
He'll NEVER steer you wrong
or let you down"

My Storyteller

Words spawn and rattle around in my head
Adhering to each other, forming sentences, forming thoughts
Stringing together a looming
Agitation,

              Sadness,

                              Dread

These words become a prison
The ink that blots the canvas of my mind
Deepens,

              Spreads,

                              Pollutes

Reaching so far and
Growing so dark
That they begin to form the very bars that confine me

The very depth of thought that forms these words has drowned
me in a sea of
Anxiety,

              Fear,

                              Despair
My feet plant themselves firmly on the ocean floor

However

Against the words that form my jail, arise the Words of my
Creator:
What binds the peak of human strength, is no match against He
who is greater

Palmer, 36

The Words of Light
Corrupt the darkness of the ink that enslaves me
The bars, they break
The ground, it shakes
A promise
I am free

The Words of Light
Collapse the "safety" of my prison
A hand approaches
As land encroaches
I'm given breath from He who has Risen!

"In the beginning was the Word, and the Word was with God,
and the Word was God"
Don't let the other *person* have you believe in the facade

The very words that hold you captive, that make you feel there's
no relief
Those same words created the universe; when God is your belief

I reach the surface. I am
Calm,
                    Confident,
                                        Joyful
And thankful that Jesus is my storyteller

Palmer, 37

Author's Account

Close your eyes with me and picture every lie the enemy has ever convinced you of. Imagine the letters and words within those sentences cascading into a pool of ink, binding together to create a jail that you've become trapped in. It feels safe for a moment, doesn't it? The mind has a way of convincing us that if we venture outside our own personal prisons that we're bound to suffer more, so why risk feeling more sorrow when we're comfortable here? What you don't realize is that many before you have served that life sentence only to die feeling sorry for themselves, with nothing to show for this life but a handful of self-hatred.

As the poem suggests, **however**, there is a key in the power of God's word[s].

Imagine now, a single teardrop of light splashing upon the railing. One second you're suffocated by silence, and in the next you hear the sounds of bars bending, creaking, and reshaping themselves until you look up and see nothing but sky: you're free. Ashore now you look back to see the pool, once drowned in darkness, is now a beacon of peace. What you do with the freedom God has given is up to you, but I pray you'll spend what little time we have left thanking God for being the one who holds the pen. Amen.

My strength won't last forever
My looks are swept away with time
My eyes grow dim as the story that is my life comes to a bitter
end
I don't walk the way I used to
I don't talk the way I used to
The ever-changing minefield of life goes on

However,
Strength from the Lord is never fading
For it stems from the joy that he gives
His love for me is never-changing
And my sins, he always forgives

My looks are inconsequential, for beauty fades away
The state of my heart truly matters, and on the Lord mine shall
stay

My eyes that see what is visible
That only see what man can do
Are blessed with the promise of a world born anew
Where body, mind, and soul are never miserable

Blessed I am to know that my spirit will one day have peace
Blessed I am to know that my earthly struggles will soon cease
Although my body moans and cries, and may sometimes
betray me

**The word of God has said "I can do ALL things, through
Christ who strengthens me"!!!**

Palmer, 39

Author's Account

Whether walking within the grace of God, or wrapped up in the ways of the world, we all endure hardships. We all grow old, frail, lose the abilities and strengths we once had in youth, and eventually pass away. It'd be easy to observe this cycle of living, losing, and dying and find no reason to continue.

The fatal flaw of a mind set on the physical is that we're bound to lose happiness, as like everything that is of this world it will inevitably decay. Joy, however, comes from the Lord and no man, woman, or child can take away what He supplies.

I pray you read this poem, refer to the scripture, and take pride in knowing you serve a God who supplants this worldly weakness with his all-encompassing power!

<u>Hope</u>

Just as fleeting as my words
Frightened by the heavy footsteps of defeat
It peeks around the corner, praying its voice won't be muffled; its
light won't be consumed by the depths of darkness that lie in the
eyes of those who have forgotten its words

Elusive as a firefly
With childlike exuberance we run, groping the air
When caught, we hope to share the beauty in our success
But before the night is over, the fire slips through our fingers,
and flies out of sight.
Happiness arose this morning, now it's time to say goodnight

However,
As happiness is laid to rest, in its wake is joy
A feeling that fumbles fear, and calmly collects confidence
No longer a prey to feast upon, but a predator of faith
Once as shallow as a pond, now as deep, and as wide as the
ocean
As shy as a geyser: peaking above the thunderclouds, breaching
the heavy wall of rain
Drops fall and become tears on the face of man
Little does he know, the night is over: no more mourning for the
sun dries up the pain
Springtime sprouts a seed from our shame
This scent that seduces even sin:

Is Hope

Palmer, 41

Author's Account

Let's take this one paragraph by paragraph:

Having hope in this world is becoming more of a myth than it is a reality. Finding it has become almost impossible as the enemy lurks around every corner trying to snuff it out, and leave us in a world with nothing but doubt.

On the off chance that you do find some slimmer, you discover that it's just as impossible to hold on to. Hope is to happiness, as affection is to feeling loved: both so dependent on one another that once your smile fades away, so too goes any reason to believe things will get better.

As the poems before this state, **however**; a conjunction of contradiction that separates fact from fiction, despair from delight, and serves to turn our reality completely on its head.

True hope is a byproduct of joy, which is a feeling of perpetual gladness that stems from knowing your circumstances are in God's hands. This type of hope supersedes our natural inclination to worry, and instills in us the confidence [faith] to believe all things are working for our good [**Romans 8:28**]. The line "as shy as a geyser", preludes the picture of one shooting into the sky as it's meant to contradict itself; it was timid at the beginning and is now in full view of the heavens, splitting the obstacle that is our own doubt [the rain]. Finally, as it hits the earth it saturates new growth leading to a spring of hope: God's hope.

Ask the Lord for **His** hope as there's no soil it can't grow in.

Palmer, 42

Power in Prayer

We are all
Shackled to satan
Arms pinned, key is lost, we all have sinned, continue to bend the
truth as we look to the cross
In bondage and behind bars
For broken hearts we failed to mend
Weighed down by visions of better decisions we could've
made… but didn't
No glint or glimmer of hope
Scars of our youth yet to heal
Feel as if we fall to all things
And fail to cope

But God

The jingle of a keychain
 For Christ holds the key to change:
To rearrange the reality of all those who believe
Bestowed with blessings, unburdened by stress,
Relieved of the pain that persists from wounds that weep from
many moons ago
Once doomed
Now mercy and grace take the place of self-hate
As the hole in your soul, and flesh once severed begins to seal
Cracked chains chip and shatter
devil and demons scatter now
Unafraid and free, lift from the pit that is despair
All can receive such gifts if you:
Trust the power of prayer

Palmer, 43

Author's Account

But God is an expression, or rather the exclamation of saying that regardless of what we may be experiencing, God **will** overcome. We may be in servitude to our own sins, jailed for all the hearts we've broken, and crippled by guilt for all the mistakes we made and could've avoided... **but God.** The phrase stands alone as you're made to ponder it, focus on it, and glean from it the true significance of what it means to trust in the power He has stored up for his family. Such power can only be given to us by solemnly and humbly asking for it in prayer.

Prayer is the gate by which we open our minds to the possibility of miracles, and what we must walk through in order to make a way for God to move.

Palmer, 44

My God is

A thrill to my senses, my God is
He speaks; the gentle lisp of his words arouse the wind
It blows a kiss my way, comforts my cheek in this sweltering
heat
As I frolic through the flora, the aroma of which quenches the
sinful stench, tickles my nose
Substituting the stench with serenity:
The perfume of peace
I see affliction insurmountable, transgressions grow
uncountable
To Him, but a handful of his wisdom rewrites my "rights"
from "wrongs", nothing he can't handle, my disgrace turns to
his delight

But a beggar with nothing to eat, with an attire in tatters,
listening on as the unrighteous mock my misfortune and in
spite of my kindness, spit at my feet
They beg of me to forsake my Lord while I starve
But they don't know my body is fortified by His joy
As I stand on what He's said, He prepares my daily bread and
pours gourds of his blood overflowing
Carves my name into the Lamb's Book of Life

Even though I walk through the valley of the shadow of death
I'm uplifted like a dove atop his breath
On solid ground, was lost as a sinner, a sheep I was found
Saved by my shepherd, won't give less than everything

Everything, my God is

Palmer, 45

Sweet as Sunrise

Such power behind the soft spoken words of our Savior
A single stitch of his garment intertwined within our minds,
patches all that is broken
To be in his presence is to bathe in a brook of milk and honey,
To be caught in a storm of his almighty power:
A shower of sanctity
Born without, blessed with more than plenty
But a penny in the cup of my character, bestowed a wealth of
wisdom, a cup overflows
His grace and mercy spill from the rim
The acrid taste of bitterness and shame
Erased
Christ's perfection: for us, a palate cleanse
What would we do without Him?
Pray my name stays pinned in the book brandished by the Lamb
So I, we, his family may walk hand in hand with our Father

Lord, may we forsake the flesh that feeds on disobedience: deny
the draw of dusk

Pray we find the strength to set our tables at dawn, and feast
upon the decadence of day, a flavor as

Sweet as Sunrise

Author's Account

"My God Is" as "Sweet as Sunrise"; these two poems combined
are one long love letter to our Lord and Savior Jesus Christ. They
detail how he feeds us when we're spiritually weak, how he
provides us solid ground to stand on in a world full of fault lines,
and how despite our transgressions his grace and mercy bless us
with a life so sweet.

I hope that when reading them tears of joy might spring from
your eyes when you discover the effect[s] he can have on, and in
your life when you surrender to Him.

Palmer, 47

Grateful

A starving soul
Sip from a stream of iniquity
Clothed, but ragged and wrapped in wrinkles:
Forged in filth
Elsewhere
A curtain in the temple tears
The Holy Spirit is set free
Finds you, finds me
Mothers and Fathers are fed scripture
Provided the power and promise in prayer
God's grace fills the space left in the stomachs of offspring
An empty plate now breaks from the weight of
His Love
A family covered in his offering
Lips that once split to dip tongues in immorality
Now speak of the immortality God grants to those who believe
Miracles are conceived
White robes of righteousness they sew
Once lost, God finds, washes us white as snow
Love, Joy, Peace, Patience, Kindness, Goodness, Faithfulness,
Gentleness, and Self-Control
Come flowing from his sleeves
Like the blood shed on the cross
Such sacrifice leaves us never at a loss for words
We're free as the birds

Unshackled that fateful day
Gleaming and
Grateful

Author's Account

Having a God capable of doing anything and everything we need him for is something we all should be grateful, and thankful for. The fact that you can hold this book, the fact that you can read these words, the fact that you have the mind to process what I'm saying: it's something so easy to feel entitled to, but it's all a blessing! It doesn't matter your circumstance, your social or economic status, who you do or don't know, what matters is you're here: you're alive! I pray you learn (if you haven't already) to cherish what you have, and thank God for it because your life could've gone in any other direction… **but God.**

Relief for the backslider

Time can be granted
Lessons, retaught
You caused the problem, but
Problems for God are naught
"Through Christ who strengthens me": Philippians 4:13
More than a simple soliloquy: He is the
Word; that speaks life into existence
Truth; get right, and live it with consistence
"Get wisdom", seek Him Proverbs 4:5, 8:17
Make Christ more than just a semblance in your life
"Take up your cross", and do it without resistance Matthew 16:24-25
Don't be caught
By the shackles of temptation
Her lips may be as sweet as honey Proverbs 3:5-6
But they rob you of salvation
A reminder: Jesus' blood was more than a simple donation
He died for you and me
To give us ALL a firm foundation:
To do good,
To live righteous,
Don't love money,
Faith is priceless
Our daily bread, we must take it Matthew 6:9-13
Our solid rock, don't let the enemy shake it Psalms 62:2

Ephesians 1:7-8 (NIV)
"In him we have redemption through his blood, the forgiveness
of sins, in accordance with the riches of God's grace 8 that he
lavished on us..."

Palmer, 50

By grace, you are redeemed
Your sins, too much they seem
His forgiveness: never ending
Don't abuse it for it's YOUR soul you're offending

Author's Account

As someone who backslides often, I've found that the enemy perverts the depression I feel in those moments to convince me to stay within my sin. In my vulnerability he persuades me to believe that it'd be better to continue on my crooked path, than to crawl my way back to the altar over and over again asking the Lord for forgiveness. Guilt and shame are then born from this depression, both of which lead me to suffer longer than I have to, causing an endless cycle of feeling sorry for myself.

The problem with that state of mind is that I hold too high an expectation for myself: I am a sinner, punishing himself for not being perfect. Although it's the enemy who latches onto our [sometimes] wretched emotions, **we** have the power to come to this realization, swallow that guilt, and move on... but we don't ... and it's because we try to do it in our own way (which is what got us stuck in the first place).

To those of us who struggle with such, this poem is for you: I pray that you don't continue to beat yourself up for being human [men and women who make mistakes], but instead follow the guidance in these words the Lord has put on my heart, and find relief in knowing there's no problem God can't fix.

Believing in a legacy

Imagine this

A child sitting in snow, with nothing but a dream to see the
seed he clutches grow
Too young to know, not the season, nor the circumstance to fix
such wide eyes on the potential teeming
A sun steady beaming
Can't seem to cause the torrential blizzard to cease
The climate churns, as child turns to teen, still wishing for a
dream

Some wonder why hope remains
Why tears, and the fears of failure don't stain the coat

Nevermind their persistence, the interests of the ignorant don't
faze the boy for unlike the swarm, he's not blind; heart stays
warm even in winter's cold
Emboldened by their insistence, young man continues to wait,
despite their hatred
Won't fight his fate:
To die before his efforts see his seedling kiss the sky

Older, even colder, yet ever so spry
Stutter step shifts to a shuffle, shuffle precedes a stumble as his
soul tumbles to the grave; nothing can save old age
To the end his spirit never splintered from his goal, ice ignites
from the cinders, a raging fire from what he felt, snow begins
to melt, no hinder: arise, a rose

Imagine that

Palmer, 53

Author's Account

A poem that took minutes to write, but weeks of brainstorming to produce. This poem is my favorite of the uplifting ones as it deals with something I feel we all, at some point in our lives, come to terms with: feeling like all our efforts are in vain. The Lord has called **me** to be a servant of man: a calling I struggle with almost daily as it's hard giving my all to a world that will reward my kindness with a slap to the face. This poem was the Lord's way of reminding me that even though His plan for me might not be fully realized, even though others may laugh, or misunderstand why I do what I do, from my efforts a rose **will** arise. For some of you, this might look like continuing to lend money to that one relative/friend when he[she] needs it, for others it may be continuing to be a friend to someone who abuses your compassion and gives you nothing in return. Whatever your passion/calling is, this is a reminder to keep watering your "seed" because the Lord will make sure that, whether you're alive or dead when it happens, you **will** receive a reward for your patience and long-suffering in due time.

Palmer, 54

Why Use Me?

I lack the ambition
I lack the drive
I dive headfirst into trouble when it's presented
Not convicted enough:
To do right,
To be honest
My pride reaches the heavens, and that's me being modest
I'm past the point of saving
Stumbling towards my future, present sins I'm still craving
For my crimes I deserve life, but when it comes time to hear the
gavel, face hits the gravel, I plead, beg so loud my ears bleed
My words deserve to fall on deaf ears
But your Holy Spirit interferes between my tears
My heart hardened by sin, given grace to begin beating for Him
again
If not for the word: "repent", my death would've been imminent,
once stumbled now I walk straight
The gift of a humble prayer that was sent
I thought I: despicable. My sins short unforgivable
While I fervently fondled filth with these hands, on the chess
board, God proceeded with his plans:
To pry me away from being a pawn, a spawn of the devil. I'm
stuck on the first floor while he sees ALL the levels

Once depressed on a dying earth, my flesh I grew to hate
I then gave my life to Jesus, and before the game begins: that's
checkmate

Palmer, 55

Author's Account

If life is a chessboard where we're all pawns tasked with serving the King of Kings or the prince of darkness, then in serving God we truly have won the game before it starts. A king that is all good, who exists outside of evil, is one that we can only benefit from as he seeks his subjects best interest at heart. Knowing this we should never be left to wonder what our purpose is, because we've already been shown that regardless of what the world throws at us, our God will protect and provide us with all the tools we need to thrive.

Calling back to **Romans 8:28**, if all things work together for our good, then what reason do we have to believe that we can't be lifted from our sin, and put on the path of righteousness? Is there anything God *can't* do within his plan to craft us into perfect people?

My prayer is that you ask yourself these questions (every day if you have to) until you realize that none of us are righteous [**Ecclesiastes 7:20**] nor will we ever truly be **BUT**... just like with David, Ruth, and Abraham, God can still turn sinful men and women into kings and faithful servants despite it all.

Thoughts and Feelings

"Patterns of negativity
we've allowed to persist at the
expense of our sanity.
May you recognize these cycles
and allow the LORD to break those chains!"

Look for yourself in these words.
Look for your reflection in these pages.
You're not alone.

Palmer, 58

A pen strokes diligently across paper
Its nib is worn down
Lead breaks,
Graphite goes to waste
On what few would consider a masterpiece
Never effortless,
The toil continues
Pigment runs like cheap eyeshadow
Streams like a river, yet like a river it dries up
Up and down the paper it scrolls
Until there's nothing left
Are we done yet?
The canvas isn't better off
Punctured,
Bruised,
Abused,
And for what!?
A mediocre coat of paint?
Creation continues
The picture, yet to be completed
A question: artist, **why aren't you defeated!?**
You paint, you draw, you sketch
The flow of time seems eternally stretched
You never put your utensil down: you even sculpt a bit
Your pens personified left to wonder: **won't you ever quit!?**
A void:
Like the hollow vessel used to paint "this perfect world"
Pray it's more than just a colorful stain when this is over

Addiction

Shower, Rinse, Repeat
Shower, Rinse, Repeat
Wake up, I hit the street
Dutifully, I follow my feet
Hands move, old souls I meet
New faces, I fail to greet
My heart never skips a beat

Never skipped a beat

Night falls, I take a seat
In filth, I fall asleep

Shower, Rinse, Repeat
Shower, Rinse, Repeat
Wake up, I hit the street
This time, I trail behind my feet
Amiss; my hands, they miss their beat
Off rhythm; new dance, my mind retreats
Skin crawls, gears turn; a sweltering heat
Cold shiver; I freeze atop concrete
Mind's gone, my senses they deplete
Out of sight, facefirst I fall upon the street
Crowds follow, all fall; an endless fleet
I shower in my addiction, step out
Rinsed down with my affliction
Daylight to nightfall; mind and soul in friction
Mind writhes in agony, my soul loses conviction

Repeat, Repeat, Repeat
Repeat, Repeat, Repeat

Palmer, 60

The ombre of day falls into night
As light shrinks away
The moon fights to keep the creeping sun at bay

It wonders why its time is so temporary
Almost scary
How quick dusk gets rushed to dawn

Man's eyes don't perceive the struggle
As darkness feels the muzzle: what it's like to be held at
gunpoint
Forced to concede your contribution to life, in bitter strife

A permanent daybreak
Warmth in abundance, look what's at stake
You'd sacrifice sleep, for sunrise?
No peace for sore eyes?
Don't mistake me for a fool

Like a lost love one, "Luna" longs for the final mist of
morning
Pray the ombre comes to a full
Stop
So it never sees the light again

Palmer, 61

Pain personified
It's not classified information
The truth is: I struggle to find elation
Your words, they cut deep
Like shark teeth: a serration
I'm paper: a perforation
My thoughts are ice, the surface of which you're
Skating
I'm flaking
My soul's the wall
Thin pieces fall, become thick
Not quite so tall anymore
I hit the floor
Now the room is missing
A peace of my mind
"It's fine"
Are you even listening?
Are my feelings too strong?
Am **I** in the wrong?
Must I sing a song, a ballad
Just to be heard?
You ask; I sing like a bird
But if my feelings were a vote,
There'd be nothing in the ballot
Box
I'm in
I seek
A friend
I'm weak
A hand to lend?
In sadness, I'm steeped
Alone again, and again, and again
Don't tell me "it's sin, it's sin". **It's sin.**

Palmer, 62

User

I ache
A constant state of heartbreak
Constantly loaning a smile
Forgiveness waives interest
Paid back in pity
To help carry your shame and sorrow
Borrow this back of mine
Bask in this light I shine upon you
My true intention:
I seek the same vision you have for yourself
To have someone willing to sacrifice what money can't buy:
Time
Trust your reason is my rhyme; sweat shines, I wind down,
tilling your crops, hope to prop you up so you can climb your
Everest
I never rest in my pursuit of your happiness

But along your quest, my willpower grows weak
Manipulate my meekness
Perpetuate my fever
Running for you in the rain 'till I'm ragged
I alone to blame
This fervor all but fleeting
Sublime on the surface, while heartbeat is depleting

The giver left with nothing but a sliver
No glimmer of what's to gain, only bane
Message remains the same:
"I live to be of service"
Taunted with the taste of an award
Death's door, my reward is to be worthless

Palmer, 63

<u>Pride</u>

We meet on the ballroom floor
Adorned in violet
Tip toes towards me with a sway so great,
It's violent
With eager hands on her hips
These words that lift off her lips
My grasp no longer meager
Her lips, red like fire
She fills my head with tales of glory
Entranced by the story, I don't realize it's a lie;
That she's a liar
Sedated by her seduction, she leads me to my own destruction

Married to her now
Locked up in a tower; she makes this house a home
Outside a garden grows: arrogance is overgrown
Was sweet, its taste turned sour

Humble beginnings come to an end, and so too my fruitful life
So glad to be surrounded by my friends and loving wife

Naive and young, he passed away; still in deception when he
died

Thought to be lifted to the Lord in peace
Autopsy reads he was put down by pride

Palmer, 64

I can't hear my footsteps
It's as if this crippled soul
Is dragging along this flesh of mine
Both wanting desperately to be whole

I can't hear my footsteps
The breeze is loud in my head
My mind is a hollow branch:
Thoughts come in, they flow out
A hollow branch is dead

I can't hear my footsteps
Blades of grass bow beneath my feet
Every step, as if I'm a king
Who feels the opposite of royalty
For grass has no mind to know
A king, a jester, a peasant…
Is anybody listening?

How would I hear my footsteps
My empty heartbeat is too loud

Palmer, 65

hatred

I thought we'd drive forever, but it seems this is her stop
Was her stop
Heart falls like the backdrop; it's no longer day
Alone, and nothing to keep *that* feeling at bay
I ride
That feeling's <u>BEEN</u> inside
The windshield cracks from my gaze, never lacks
Intensity
I fight the wheel, it won't fight back
Headlights fume
This fire looms in immensity
The horn masks the sounds of my screams
Radio silence, once was music, now that feels like a dream
The tank's on empty, I wished for plenty, the car coasts but
soon will die
Seatbelt grows stiff
Car meets cliff
I fall to my death and cry:
"NOTHING IS SACRED"
Cliff meets bottom; I drown
I'm surrounded by
hatred

Palmer, 66

What am I?
Take a guess. A hint: there lies no pride in my chest

Confidence eludes me
Weak winds make me waver like a leaf
Life's a freezer, a child chatters at their teeth
Meet my lover, her name's Uncertainty

Steady chatter
Makes me feel there's no relief
I'm broken, can't you see?
These thoughts won't let me be!
I take solace in my self-imposed grief

Nobody sees me, I steadily ask why
We live in my head, let's take a tour
Uncertainty and I; I **think** our love is pure
A son; he's named "Anxiety" and unprovoked, he'll cry

My sadness is a sickness, there seems to be no cure
Anxiety grows older, it seems he'll never die
I tell myself that "I can do this"; I tell myself a lie
I've caught up to confidence, my grip still so unsure
I know I sound like a pest
Have you guessed?

I'm insecure

Palmer, 67

Love

I open the door and she steps inside
We ride
The drive feels like forever
I'd be blessed to make this feeling my bride
Our windshield like no other plays memories; our favorite
movie
Our stereo beats like our hearts, a tune that's oh so groovy
Strap in, it gets so much better
The road, it bumps, it turns, it winds
As well, the chemistry of our minds
We jerk sometimes, still intertwined; the feeling stays sublime
She wants to drive, I let her
Gauge never drops, we never stop
The gas, our hearts are full
No journey's end
My "bestest" friend
We ride
On to the future
She is
I am
We are in
Love

Palmer, 68

Author's Account

I wanted to allow you to read each poem and find your own meaning in it before I swooped in and said otherwise. Most don't require explanation but for the ones that may be confusing, here's the explanation:

"A pen strokes diligently across paper…" We are God's chosen utensils that he uses to mold and shape the world in his image. Though it's a blessing to be chosen, it doesn't come without hardship. This poem compares said hardship to that of being a pen/pencil worn down without knowing what the point of it being used so heavily is. Instead of being uplifting however, it highlights the reality of feeling like it's all pointless because we can't see the full picture.

"The ombre of day falls into night…" is about having the self-control to choose "the moon" over "the sun". Inspired by my relationship, I wrote it out of guilt for the feelings I had for another woman, whilst being engaged. My love for my fiancé is the moon, while the other woman is the sun, with the poem itself being me pleading with my spirit to let those feelings go so that I may have peace.

"Pride…" Following the story you'll notice the man [humanity] begins as someone too timid to properly hold the feeling, but as the dance continues not only does he grow more sure of himself, but he grows blind to the fact that "she" is poisoning him. By the story's end, he's so captivated by "her", so full of himself, that he doesn't realize how far gone from the truth he is.

"Pain personified…" The final, **"It's sin"** is bolded to draw your attention to the fact that despite the heartbreak in these words, it's sin: that it's the enemy perpetuating the pain.

Palmer, 69

Lord, **Help Me.**

"The mirror of my soul is stained with these
words of weakness and I don't have the strength
to look away. Close my eyes to what the world
wants me to see, and allow them to be opened,
and made aware of the promises you have for
me. Position my feet so that instead of being
glued in place, they might pursue you; that I
may draw nearer to your face.
Erase my sins, cleanse my soul,
Straighten my path of laziness
I need you, Lord, to be whole.
Amen."

Palmer, 70

www.ingramcontent.com/pod-product-compliance
Lightning Source LLC
Chambersburg PA
CBHW070828100426
42813CB00003B/538